ESSENTIAL ELEMENTS

FOR STRINGS

A COMPREHENSIVE STRING METHOD

MICHAEL ALLEN • ROBERT GILLESPIE • PAMELA TELLEJOHN HAYES
ARRANGEMENTS BY JOHN HIGGINS

These piano accompaniments can provide helpful guidance for teaching beginning string players. The format includes a cue line to provide the teacher or pianist with a visual guide of the student melody part.

The accompaniments have been arranged to match the style and harmony of the accompaniments heard on the play-along CDs. They may be used for teaching or performance and offer a variety of styles, from classical to contemporary popular music. You may want to alter these piano accompaniments to meet your specific needs. Chord symbols are provided.

ISBN 978-0-634-05270-5

HAL•LEONARD®
CORPORATION
7777 W. BLUEMOUND RD. P.O. BOX 13819 MILWAUKEE, WI 53213

D MAJOR

1. TUNING TRACK

2. D MAJOR SCALE – Round   *(When group A reaches ②, group B begins at ①)*

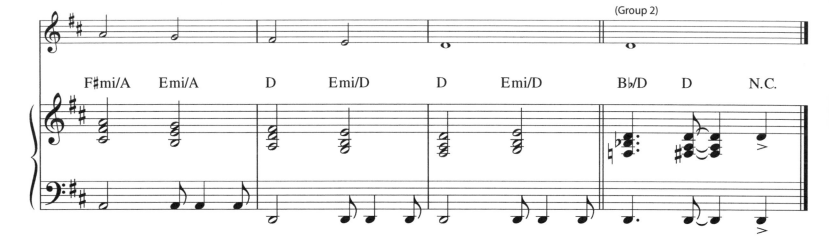

3. D MAJOR ARPEGGIO

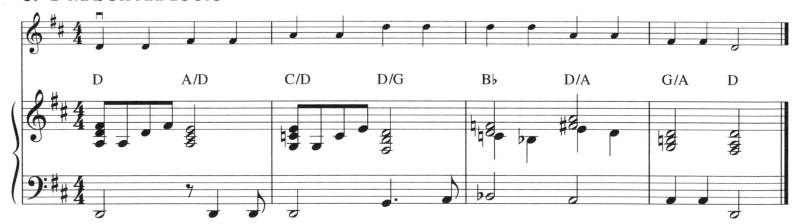

4. D MAJOR MANIA

D MAJOR

5. THEME FROM LONDON SYMPHONY

Franz J. Haydn (1732–1809)

6. D MAJOR IN THREES

3/4 RHYTHMS

7. DYNAMIC CONTRASTS

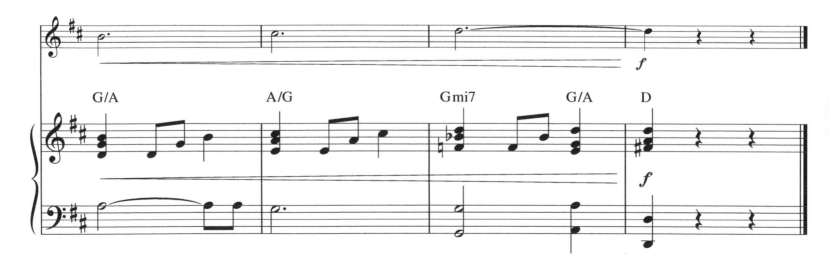

8. MORNING (from Peer Gynt)

Edvard Grieg (1843–1907)

9. BARCAROLLE

Jacques Offenbach (1819–1880)

3/4 RHYTHMS

G MAJOR

10. G MAJOR SCALE – Round

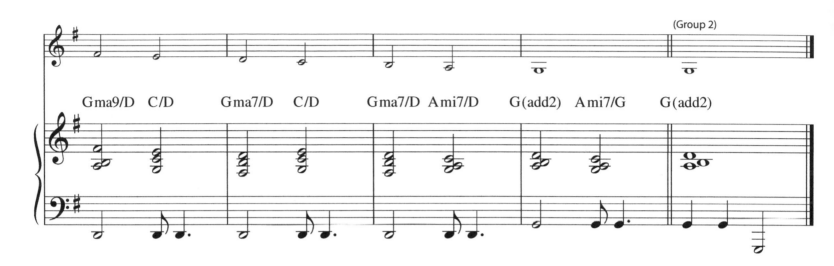

11. G MAJOR ARPEGGIO

12. SCALE INTERVALS

G MAJOR

13. CHESTER

William Billings (1746–1800)

14. G MAJOR SCALE

15. G MAJOR ARPEGGIO

G MAJOR

16. INTONATION ENCOUNTER – Duet

17. THE OUTBACK

18. C MAJOR SCALE

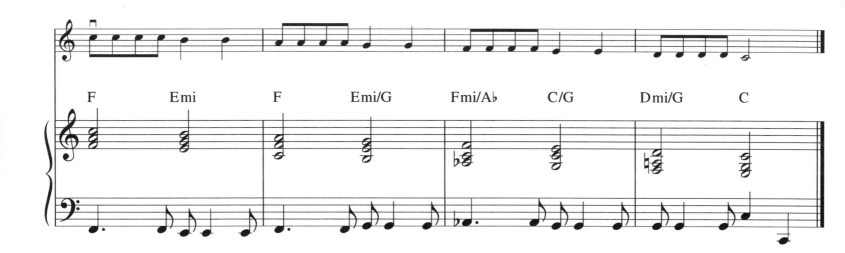

19. C MAJOR ARPEGGIO

20. C MAJOR DUET

21. BUFFALO GALS

Cool White (John Hodges)

C MAJOR

22. C MAJOR SCALE – Round

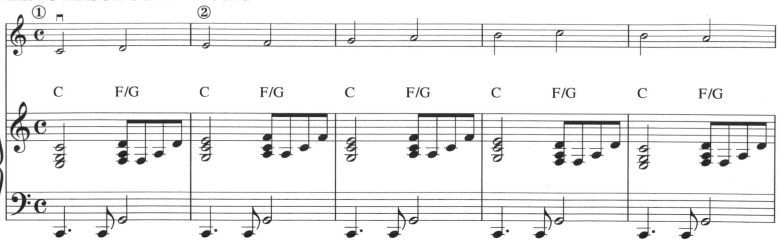

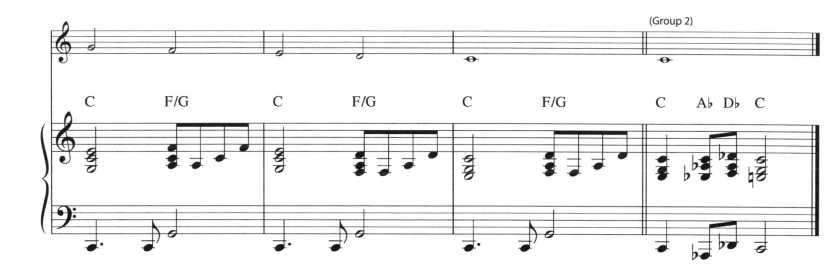

23. C MAJOR ARPEGGIO

24. C MAJOR MANIA

25. CROSSROADS

Moderato

26. THE DOT ALWAYS COUNTS

Student books have repeats after 4 bars.

27. ALOUETTE

Allegretto

French Folk Song

28. RIGAUDON

Henry Purcell (1659–1695)

29. ESSENTIAL CREATIVITY – OH! SUSANNAH

Stephen C. Foster (1826–1864)

30. RHYTHM RAP ♪ ⁊

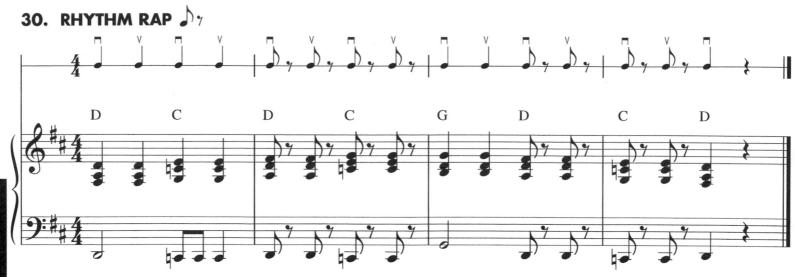

31. EIGHTH NOTES ON THE BEAT

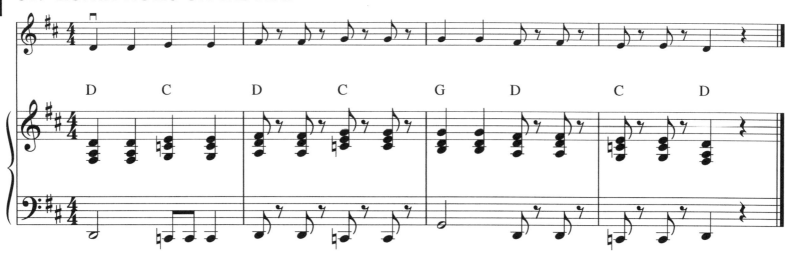

32. SHORT AND SWEET

Student books have repeats, not 1st and 2nd endings.

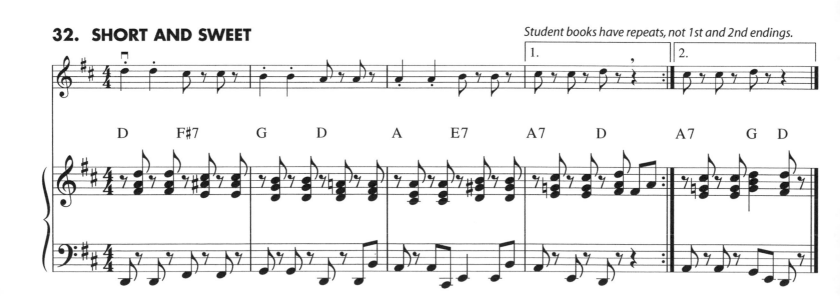

RHYTHMS

33. RHYTHM RAP

RHYTHMS

34. EIGHTH NOTES OFF THE BEAT

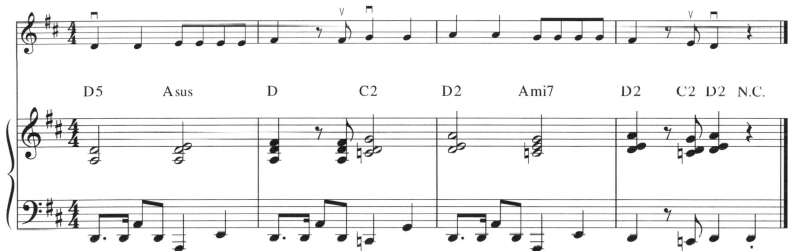

35. SUNNY DAY

36. ESSENTIAL ELEMENTS QUIZ – JESSE JAMES

Folk Ballad from Missouri

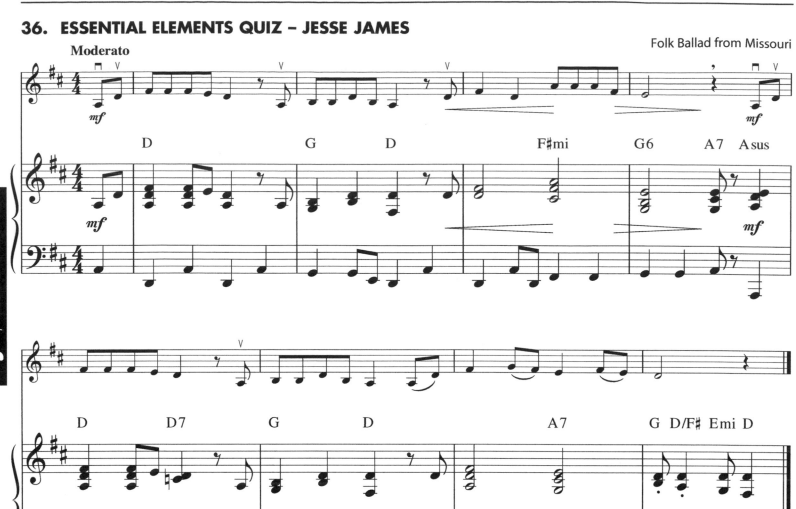

RHYTHMS

37. RHYTHM RAP

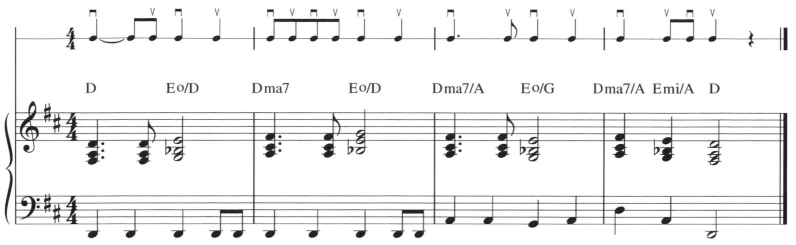

38. THE DOT COUNTS

39. WATCH THE DOT

Student books have repeats, not 1st and 2nd endings.

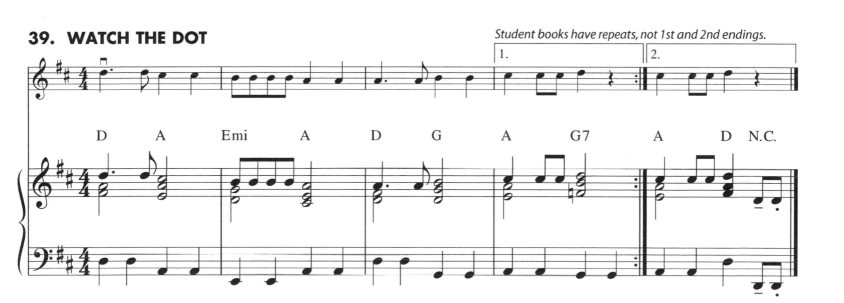

RHYTHMS

40. D MAJOR SEQUENCE

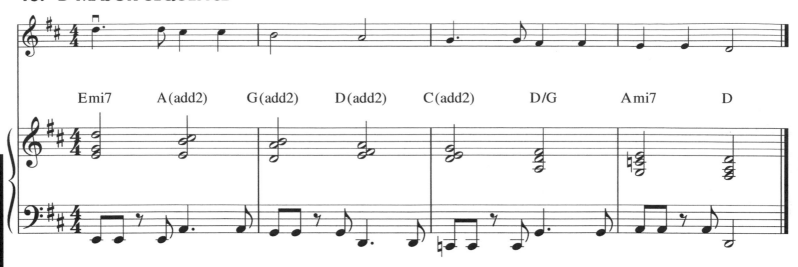

Emi7   A(add2)   G(add2)   D(add2)   C(add2)   D/G   Ami7   D

41. DOTS ON THE MOVE

D   A7   D   Bmi   Emi7 A7   D

42. D MAJOR BONANZA – Duet

Bmi   F#mi   G   Dsus   D   Emi   D/A   A7sus   A7   D

43. A CAPITAL SHIP

Moderato

American Folk Song

44. ESSENTIAL CREATIVITY

45. HOOKED ON DOTS

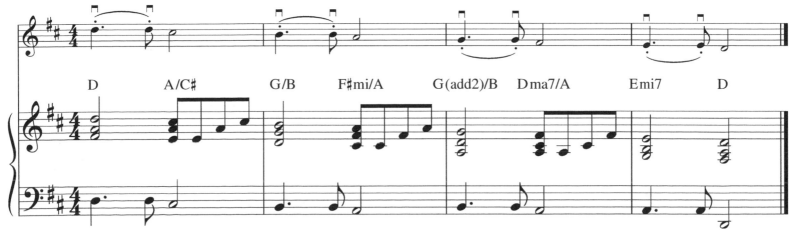

46. THEME FROM NEW WORLD SYMPHONY

Antonin Dvorák (1841–1904)

47. ESSENTIAL ELEMENTS QUIZ – RONDEAU

Jean-Joseph Mouret (1682–1738)

SHARP KEYS

48. LET'S READ "C♯" (C-sharp)

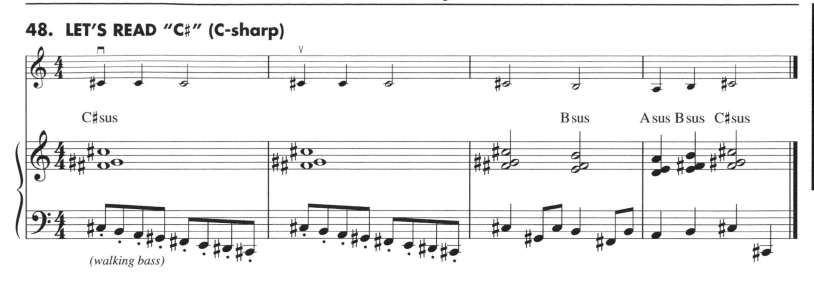

(walking bass)

C♯sus   Bsus   Asus Bsus C♯sus

49. STAY SHARP

A   E   A   D   A   E   A

50. AT PIERROT'S DOOR

French Folk Song
Student books have repeats, not 1st and 2nd endings.

Andante

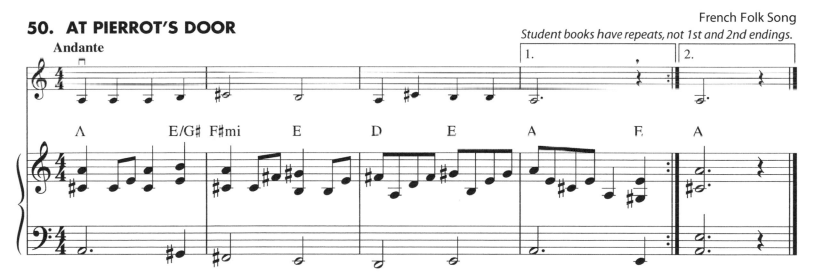

A   E/G♯ F♯mi   E   D   E   A   E   A

51. HOT CROSS BUNS

Moderato

A   E   A   E   A   D   E   A   E   A

SHARP KEYS

52. LET'S READ "G♯" (G-sharp)

53. REACHING OUT

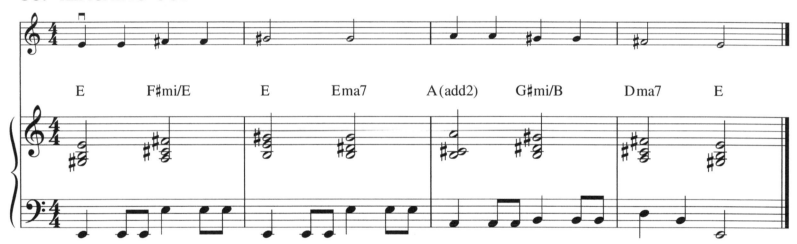

54. HIGHER AND HIGHER

SHARP KEYS

55. A MAJOR SCALE

56. ESSENTIAL ELEMENTS QUIZ – A SONG FOR ANNE

SHARP KEYS

57. LET'S READ "F#" (F-sharp) – Review

58. HIGH POINT

59. MAGNIFICENT MONTANA

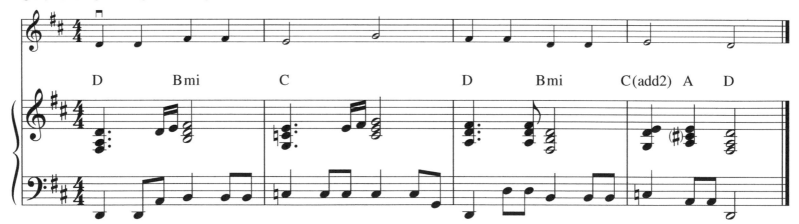

60. D MAJOR SCALE – Round

(Group 2)

A7　G7　A7　G7　D7　G13　D7　G13　B♭9　D7

61. RUSSIAN FOLK TUNE

Allegretto

D　　Emi　D/F♯　G　D/F♯　G　　　D/F♯　D

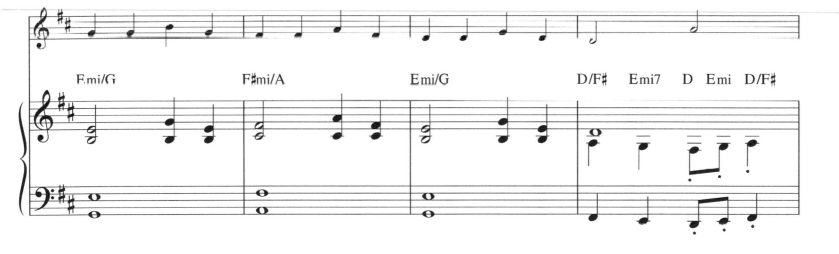

Emi/G　　F♯mi/A　　Emi/G　　D/F♯　Emi7　D　Emi　D/F♯

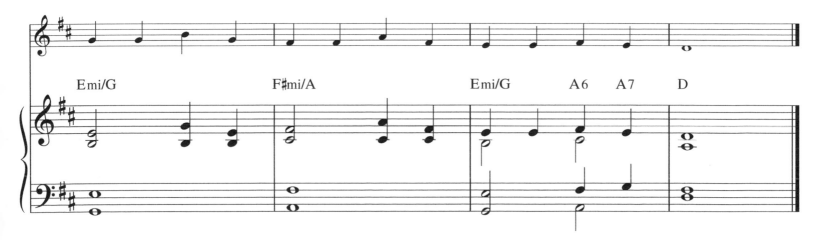

Emi/G　　F♯mi/A　　Emi/G　　A6　A7　　D

SHARP KEYS

62. LET'S READ "G♯" (G-sharp)

63. A MAJOR SCALE

64. A MAJOR ARPEGGIO

65. THE FIG TREE

66. SITKA CITY

Russian Folk Song

RHYTHMS

67. RHYTHM RAP

Student books have repeats, not 1st and 2nd endings.

68. SIXTEENTH NOTE FANFARE

Student books have repeats, not 1st and 2nd endings.

69. TECHNIQUE TRAX

70. DINAH WON'T YOU BLOW YOUR HORN

Allegretto

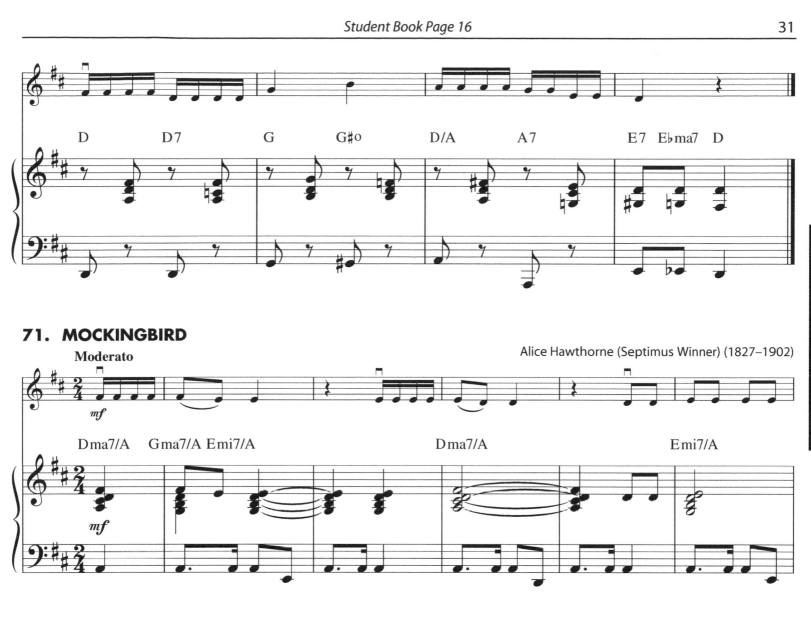

71. MOCKINGBIRD

Alice Hawthorne (Septimus Winner) (1827–1902)

72. RHYTHM RAP

Student books have repeats, not 1st and 2nd endings.

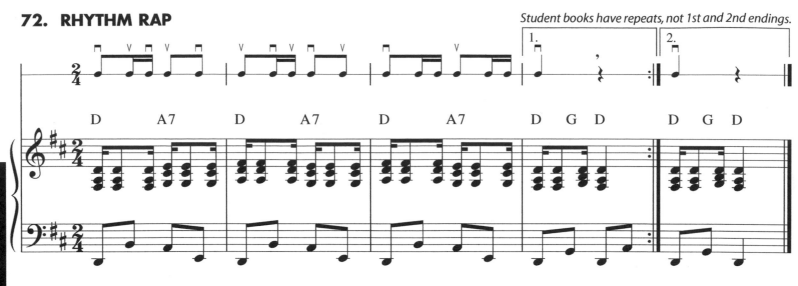

73. BLUEBERRY PIE

Student books have repeats, not 1st and 2nd endings.

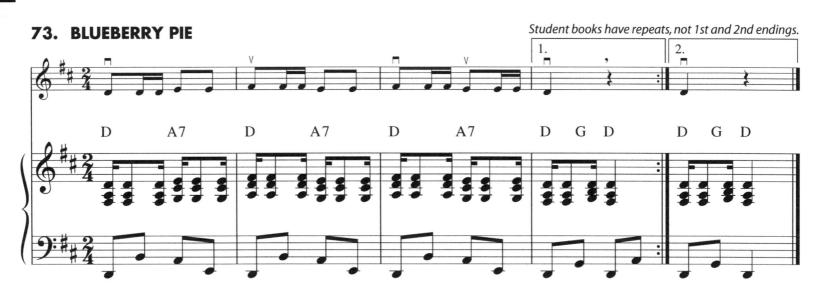

74. TECHNIQUE TRAX

RHYTHMS

75. RHYTHM RAP

Student books have repeats, not 1st and 2nd endings.

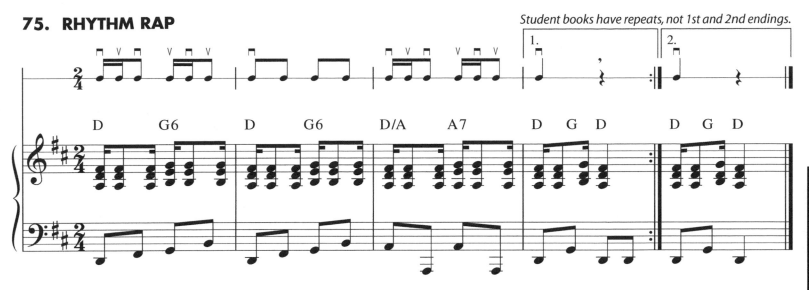

76. MARCHING ALONG

Student books have repeats, not 1st and 2nd endings.

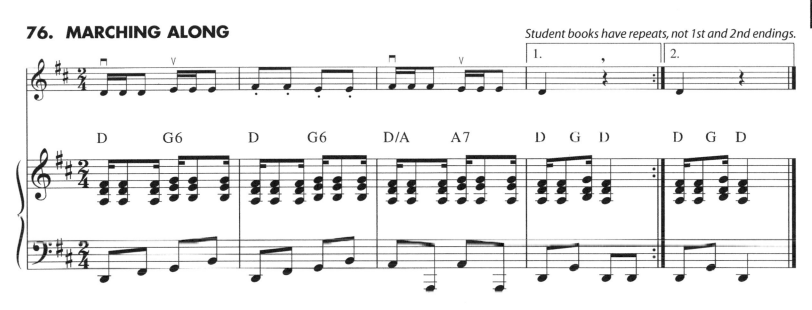

77. ON THE MOVE

RHYTHMS

78. RHYTHM ETUDE – Duet

79. ESSENTIAL ELEMENTS QUIZ – RHYTHM ROUND-UP

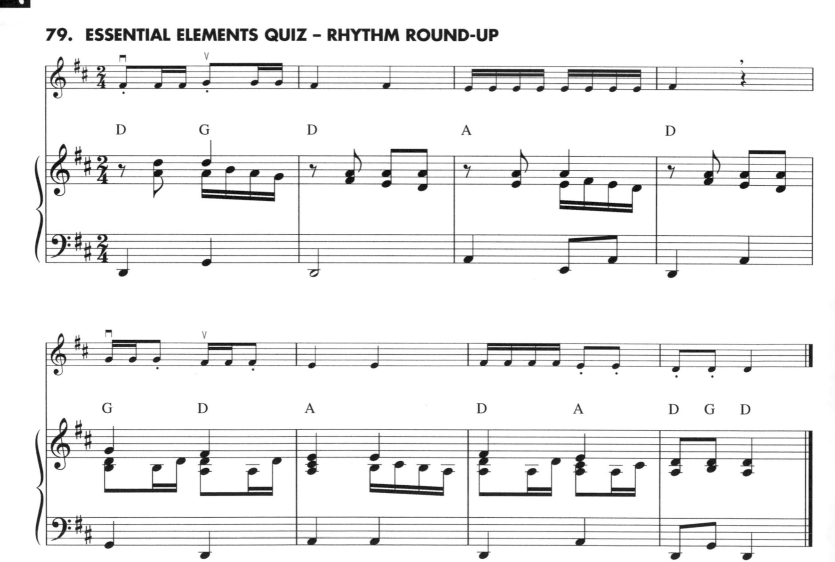

80. RHYTHM RAP

Student books have repeats, not 1st and 2nd endings.

81. TECHNIQUE TRAX

Student books have repeats, not 1st and 2nd endings.

82. HOOKED ON D MAJOR

J.J RHYTHMS

83. THE MOUNTAIN CLIMBER

84. KEEP IT SHORT

85. ESSENTIAL CREATIVITY – writing assignment in student books.

RHYTHMS

86. RHYTHM RAP

Student books have repeats, not 1st and 2nd endings.

87. SYNCOPATION TIME

Student books have repeats, not 1st and 2nd endings.

88. MIRROR IMAGE

89. CHILDREN'S SHOES

Black American Spiritual

90. HOOKED ON SYNCOPATION

91. ESSENTIAL ELEMENTS QUIZ – TOM DOOLEY

Moderato

American Folk Song

92. LET'S READ "B♭" (B-flat)

FLAT KEYS

93. ROLLING ALONG

Moderato

94. MATCHING OCTAVES

FLAT KEYS

95. LET'S READ "F" (F-natural)

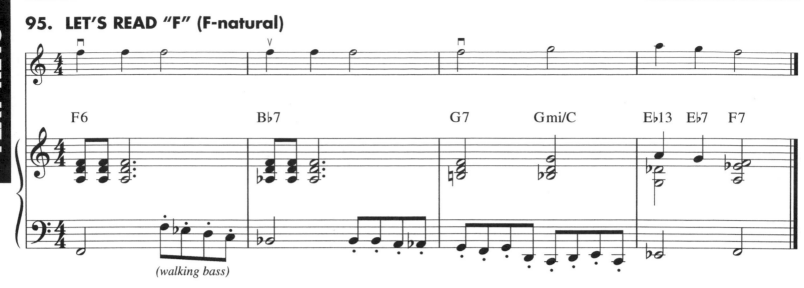

(walking bass)

96. TECHNIQUE TRAX

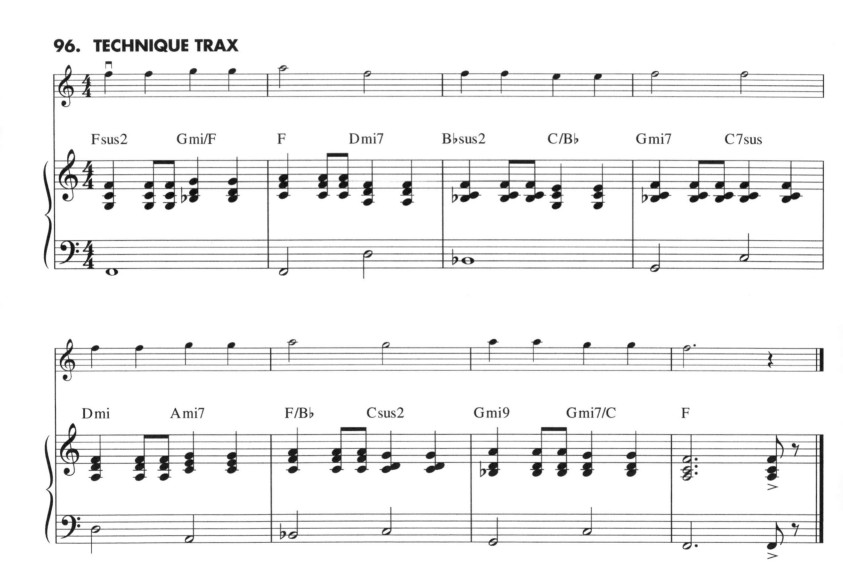

97. F MAJOR SCALE

98. THEME FROM VIOLIN CONCERTO

Ludwig van Beethoven (1770–1827)

FLAT KEYS

99. LET'S READ "E♭" (E-flat)

100. HOT CROSS BUNS

101. LET'S READ "B♭" (B-flat)

102. VIKING WAY

103. HIKING ALONG

104. B♭ MAJOR SCALE

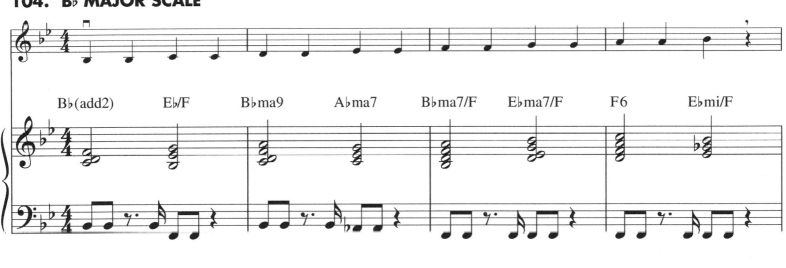

FLAT KEYS

105. SLOVAKIAN FOLK SONG

Allegro

106. CAVALIER COUNTRY

107. ESSENTIAL ELEMENTS QUIZ – AYN KAYLOKAYNU

Traditional Jewish Song

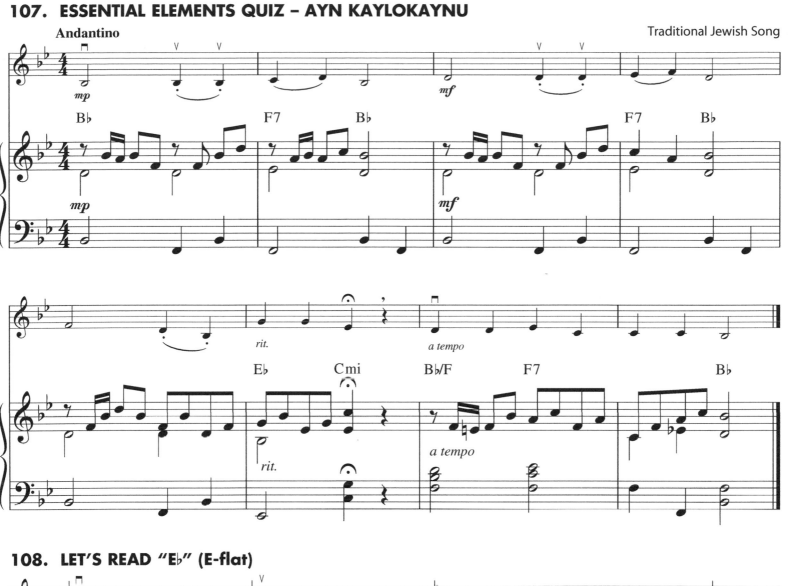

108. LET'S READ "E♭" (E-flat)

109. TECHNIQUE TRAX

FLAT KEYS

110. LET'S READ "B♭" (B-flat)

111. TECHNIQUE BUILDER

112. B♭ MAJOR SCALE

113. THE MOUNTAIN DEER CHASE

Allegretto

North American Folk Song

FLAT KEYS

FLAT KEYS

114. ESSENTIAL CREATIVITY – RAKES OF MALLOW

Irish Folk Song

115. RHYTHM RAP

116. LAZY DAY

6/8 RHYTHMS

117. HOOKED ON 6/8

118. ROW, ROW, ROW YOUR BOAT – Round

American Folk Round

(Repeat as needed for round)

119. SLURRING IN 6/8 TIME

6/8 RHYTHMS

6/8 RHYTHMS

120. JOLLY GOOD FELLOW

121. RHYTHM RAP

122. RISE AND FALL

123. BEACH WALK

124. MAY TIME

W. A. Mozart (1756–1791)

125. D MINOR (Natural) SCALE

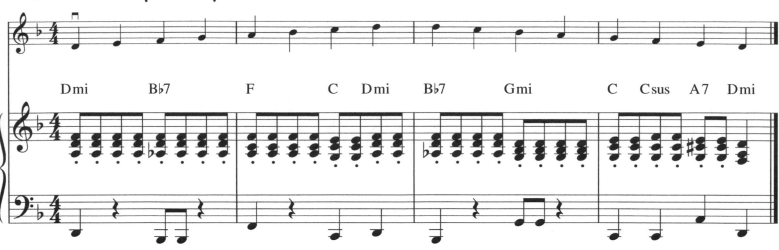

126. MAHLER'S THEME – Round

Andante

Gustav Mahler (1860–1911)

(Repeat as needed for round)

MINOR KEYS

127. SHALOM CHAVERIM – Round

Hebrew Folk Song

128. THE SNAKE CHARMER

129. G MINOR (Natural) SCALE

130. HATIKVAH

Israeli National Anthem

Student books have repeats, not 1st and 2nd endings.

Student books have repeats, not 1st and 2nd endings.

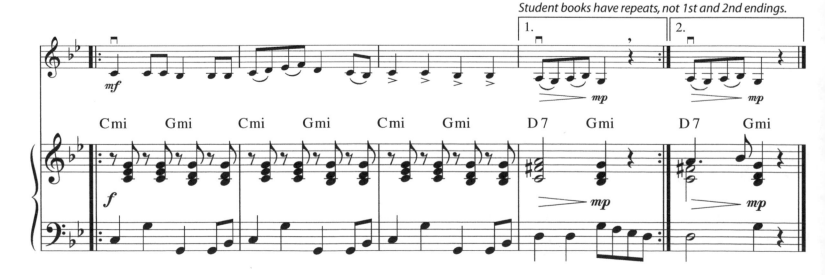

131. G MINOR (Natural) SCALE *(Upper Octave)*

132. ESSENTIAL ELEMENTS QUIZ – THE HANUKKAH SONG

Israeli Folk Song

133. RHYTHM RAP

MIXED METER

134. FRENCH FOLK SONG

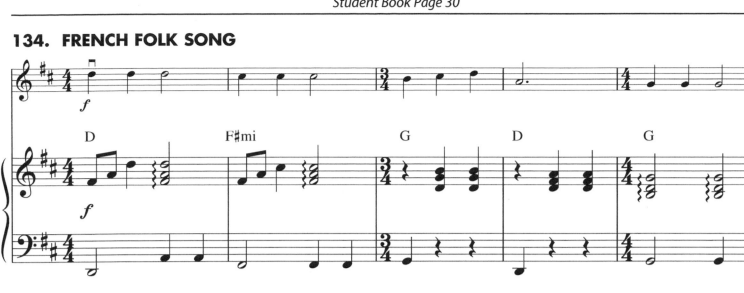

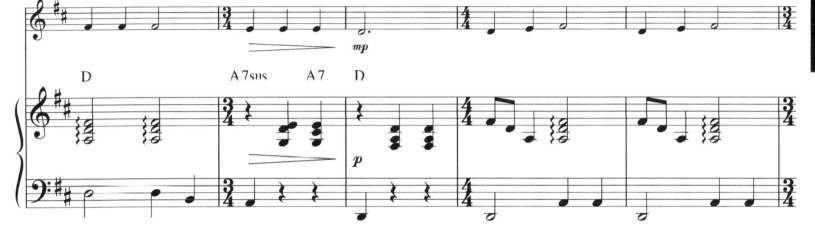

MIXED METER

135. KUM BA YAH

Andante e cantabile

African Spiritual

MIXED METER

136. RHYTHM RAP

137. D MAJOR SCALE WITH TRIPLETS

138. ON THE MOVE

139. SLURRING TRIPLETS

140. TRIPLET ETUDE

141. LITTLE RIVER

142. FIELD SONG

Moderato

Southern American Folk Song

143. RHYTHM RAP

144. A CUT ABOVE

145. CUT TIME MARCH

RHYTHMS

146. RHYTHM RAP

147. SYNCOPATION MARCH

 RHYTHMS

148. WHEN THE SAINTS GO MARCHIN' IN

James M. Black

149. RHYTHM RAP

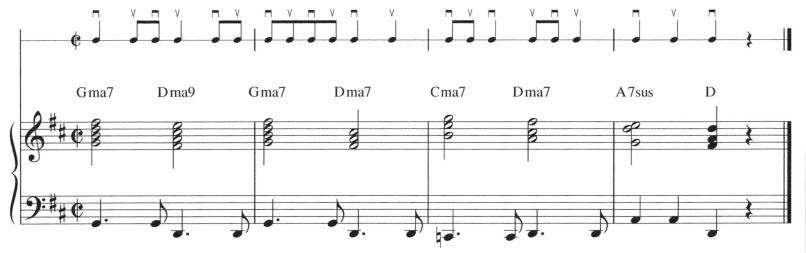

150. DOWN HOME

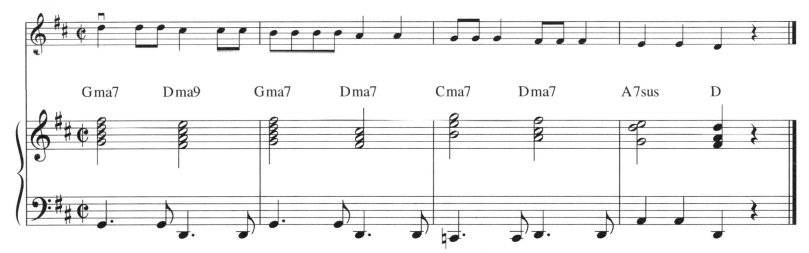

151. MOVING ALONG

152. RHYTHM RAP

153. UP TOWN

154. FLYING BOWS

155. MARCH FROM PEASANT'S CANTATA

J. S. Bach (1685–1750)

156. SAGEBRUSH OVERTURE – Orchestra Arrangement

Arr. John Higgins

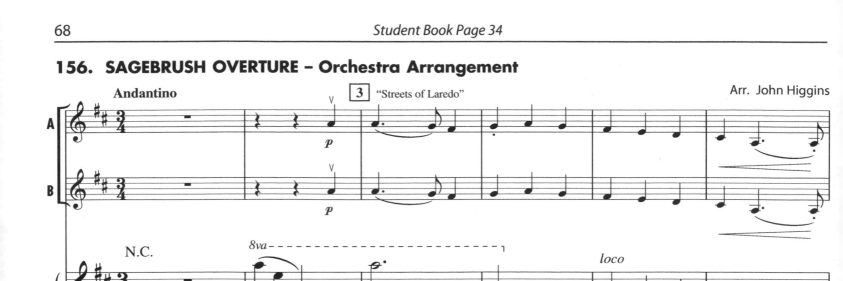

PERFORMANCE SPOTLIGHT

D   Emi/G   D/A   Emi/A   A   D/F♯   Emi7

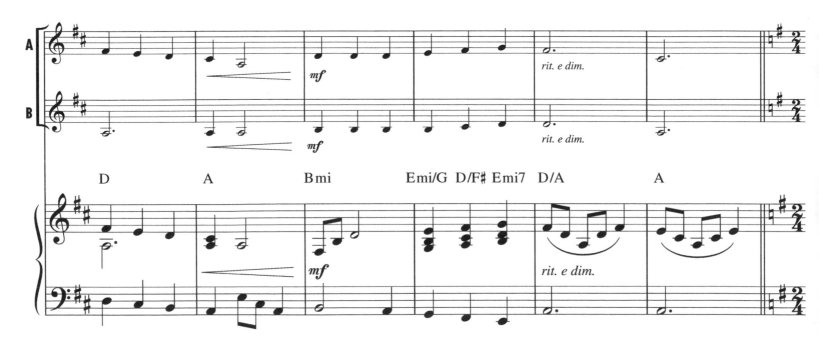

D   A   Bmi   Emi/G D/F♯ Emi7 D/A   A

Allegretto

23 "Yellow Rose of Texas"

157. POMP AND CIRCUMSTANCE – Orchestra Arrangement

Edward Elgar (1857–1933)
Arr. John Higgins

158. AMERICA THE BEAUTIFUL – Orchestra Arrangement

Samuel Augustus Ward (1847–1903)
Arr. John Higgins

159. LA BAMBA – Duet

Mexican Folk Song
Arr. Michael Allen

160. IN THE BLEAK MIDWINTER – Orchestra Arrangement

Gustav Holst (1874–1934)
Arr. John Higgins

161. SWALLOWTAIL JIG – Orchestra Arrangement

Irish Jig
Arr. John Higgins

PERFORMANCE SPOTLIGHT

162. SIGHT-READING CHALLENGE #1

163. SIGHT-READING CHALLENGE #2

164. SIGHT-READING CHALLENGE #3

165. SIGHT-READING CHALLENGE #4

166.

167.

168.

169.

HARMONICS/SHIFTING

174. 3–4 PATTERN

175. 2–3 PATTERN

176. 1–2 PATTERN

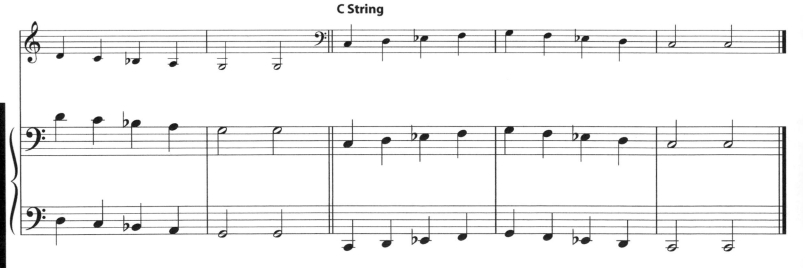

177. OPEN PATTERN

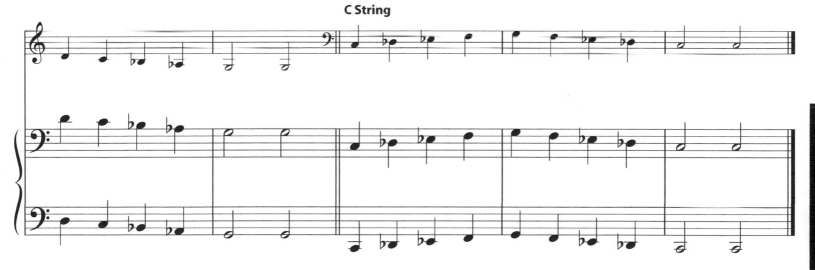

178. E STRING

179. A STRING

180. D STRING

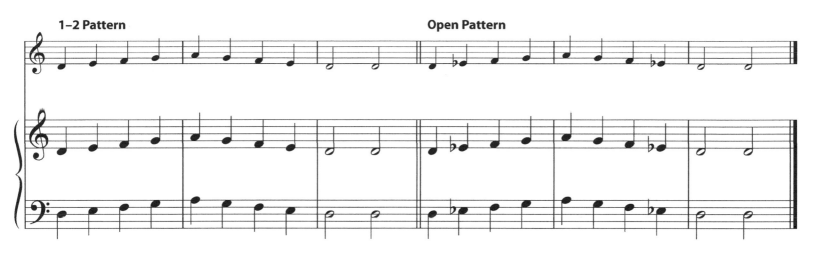

181. G STRING

FINGER PATTERNS

182. C STRING

183. C MAJOR

184. G MAJOR

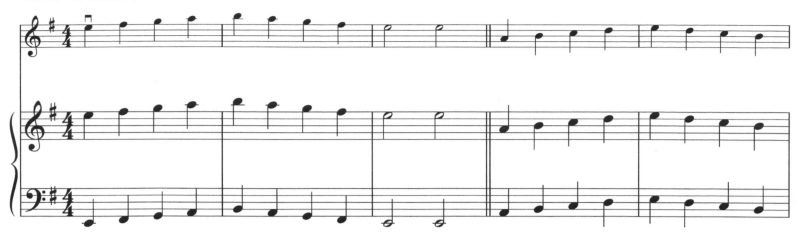

185. D MAJOR

186. A MAJOR

FINGER PATTERNS

187. F MAJOR

188. B♭ MAJOR

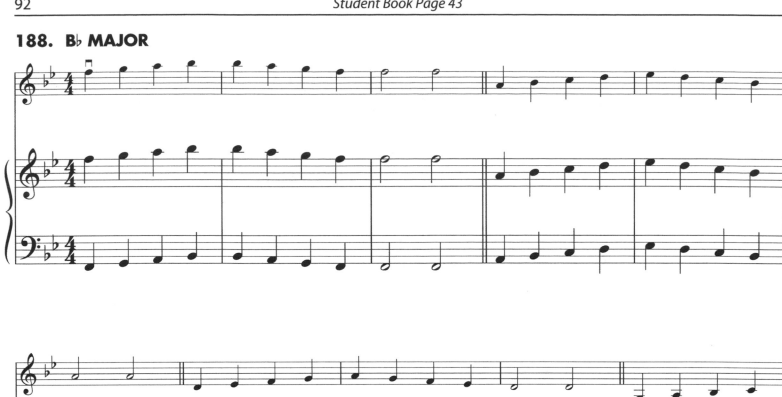

189. C MAJOR

190. C MAJOR

191. G MAJOR

192. G MAJOR

SCALES AND ARPEGGIOS

193. D MAJOR

194. D MAJOR

195. A MAJOR

196. A MAJOR

197. F MAJOR

198. B♭ MAJOR

199. B♭ MAJOR

200. D MINOR (Natural)

SCALES AND ARPEGGIOS

201. D MINOR (Natural)

202. G MINOR (Natural)

203. G MINOR (Natural)

SCALES AND ARPEGGIOS

204. – *Students improvise melody (line A) to go with accompaniment (line B).*

205. ODE TO JOY (Ludwig van Beethoven (1770–1827) – *Student books have a composition exercise.*

206. PHRASE BUILDERS – *Student books have a composition exercise.*

207. Q. AND A. – *Student books have a composition exercise.*

208. YOU NAME IT: – *Student books have a composition exercise.*

209. TWO AT A TIME

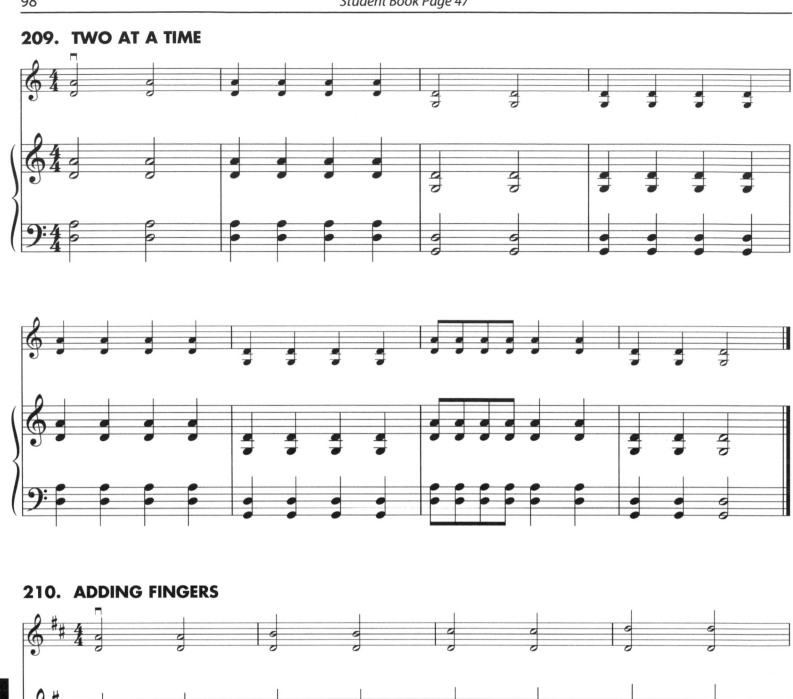

210. ADDING FINGERS

DOUBLE STOPS/FINGERING CHART

Notes

Notes